I0531177

Positive Influence for Future Impact

Daily Impact Affirmation Calendar

Dr. Nigel L. Walker

Copyright © 2026 by Nigel L Walker All rights reserved. No part of this book may be reproduced in any manner whatsoever without written permission except in the case of brief quotations embodied in critical articles and reviews. First Printing, 2026

January 01

Start your day with the intention to make a difference.

January 02

Greet the world with warmth—it changes everything.

January 03

Let your values guide your every move today.

January 04

Pause. Breathe. Respond with intention, not impulse.

January 05

Listen fully—someone's truth lives in their words.

January 06

Own your mistakes— they build the strongest bridges.

January 07

Encourage boldly. Your words might be the turning point.

January 08

Be on time, be prepared—be the one they can count on.

January 09

Replace complaints with solutions and watch what shifts.

January 10

Presence is the most powerful gift you can give.

January 11

Patience in frustration is power in disguise.

January 12

Gratitude turns ordinary moments into gold.

January 13

Take a moment before you react—it changes everything.

January 14

Kindness over convenience. Always.

January 15

Consistency in attitude builds the deepest trust.

January 16

Speak with purpose, not volume.

January 17

Celebrate wins quietly —with humility as your anthem.

January 18

Believe in someone until they believe in themselves.

January 19

Integrity is what you do when no one's watching.

January 20

Small dependable acts lead to great influence.

January 21

Choose optimism. Watch your world change.

January 22

Offer grace. It transforms judgment into connection.

January 23

A kept promise is a thread of trust.

January 24

Your attitude sets the tone—choose it wisely.

January 25

Lead through example, not just instruction.

January 26

Choose consistency, even when it's inconvenient.

January 27

Encouragement defuses tension and invites peace.

January 28

Tone speaks before words—let it be kind.

Positive Influence for Future Impact

January 29

End your day in gratitude. Always.

January 30

Reflect on your journey—growth lives in the quiet moments.

January 31

Tomorrow, show up again as a positive force.

February 01

Use someone's name —it reminds them they matter.

February 02

Check in—hearts often speak beneath the surface.

February 03

Appreciation is a gift that never returns empty.

February 04

Listen so others feel truly heard.

February 05

Serve without being asked—it speaks volumes.

February 06

Validation builds bridges stronger than advice.

February 07

Empathy over efficiency—people first, always.

February 08

Repair is an act of courage and love.

February 09

Celebrate others' success—it's a win for all.

February 10

Kindness can soften any disagreement.

February 11

Speak truth, but wrap it in compassion.

February 12

Support begins with a simple question: How can I help?

February 13

Recognize effort—it's where growth begins.

February 14

Consistency is the foundation of deep trust.

February 15

*Be approachable.
Your energy invites
connection.*

February 16

Patience with differences is the path to understanding.

February 17

Forgiveness frees the giver even more than the receiver.

February 18

Teamwork turns individual efforts into collective success.

February 19

Affirm someone's worth—watch confidence rise.

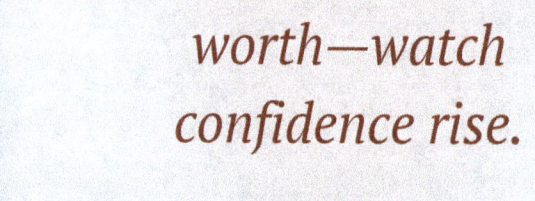

February 20

Create spaces where honesty feels safe.

February 21

Mentor with your presence, not just your advice.

February 22

Growth takes time—
be patient with it.

February 23

Advocate for others— it builds equity and courage.

February 24

Understanding begins where assumptions end.

February 25

Compassion eases tension and invites calm.

February 26

Strengthen one key relationship—it starts a ripple.

February 27

Empathy is a choice that transforms connection.

February 28

Relationships shape influence—nurture them.

March 01

Reconnect with your 'why'—let it guide your day.

March 02

Share hope—it's the first step toward possibility.

March 03

Align small actions with big dreams.

March 04

Where there is belief,
doubt fades.

March 05

*Clarity of purpose
inspires motion.*

March 06

Let your example speak louder than your words.

March 07

Ask what could be, not what's holding you back.

March 08

*Choose courage—
even when comfort
whispers.*

March 09

Model hope—it leads others through fog.

March 10

Help someone rediscover their why.

March 11

Connect the daily grind to the bigger mission.

March 12

Speak with vision.
Create momentum.

March 13

Endurance is the voice that says 'keep going.'

March 14

Stay anchored in your values under pressure.

March 15

Inspire through story —it awakens possibility.

March 16

Progress, no matter how small, is worth celebrating.

March 17

Invite others into the dream—it multiplies impact.

Positive Influence for Future Impact

March 18

Act boldly in line with your purpose.

March 19

Substance over image. Always.

March 20

When we believe together, we achieve together.

March 21

Let your vision guide your daily decisions.

March 22

Recommit to what matters most.

March 23

Pause to understand —connection begins there.

March 24

Kindness protects what arguments can't reach.

March 25

Be a voice for the voiceless.

March 26

Presence is the most healing gift.

March 27

Reassurance is often more powerful than advice.

March 28

Let compassion lead under pressure.

March 29

Create belonging where none existed before.

March 30

Acknowledging someone's story builds trust.

March 31

Choose inclusion, even if it stretches you.

April 01

Courage stands where silence used to sit.

April 02

Growth deserves patience.

April 03

Listen deeply—with no need to defend.

April 04

Grace opens doors that judgment slams shut.

April 05

Validate their struggle—it strengthens resilience.

April 06

Emotional safety invites authenticity.

April 07

Be the calm in the storm.

April 08

Unity strengthens more than agreement.

April 09

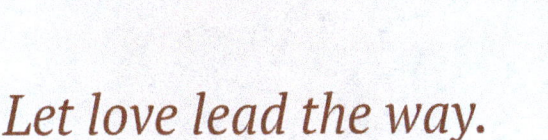

Let love lead the way.

April 10

*Build bridges—
someone is waiting on
the other side.*

April 11

Do the right thing— especially when unseen.

April 12

Own your choices— they define your character.

April 13

Make your words match your actions.

April 14

*Admit mistakes—it's
a sign of strength.*

April 15

Consistency is credibility in action.

April 16

Choose ethics over ease.

April 17

Accountability sharpens who you become.

April 18

Transparency builds trust.

April 19

*High standards
protect deep integrity.*

April 20

Speak truth—especially when it's hard.

April 21

Principles outlast popularity.

April 22

Repair trust with effort and care.

April 23

Let dependability be your reputation.

April 24

Protect your integrity —intentionally.

April 25

Self-discipline grows silent strength.

April 26

Let your character speak when you can't.

April 27

Honor every commitment fully.

April 28

Reflect on your character—it shapes your legacy.

April 29

*Lead with integrity—
it multiplies
influence.*

April 30

Ethical leadership sustains lasting impact.

May 01

Face adversity with quiet strength.

May 02

Every setback holds a lesson.

May 03

Encouragement lifts more than solutions.

May 04

Patience is perseverance in disguise.

May 05

*Rest isn't quitting—
it's recharging.*

May 06

Slow progress is still progress.

May 07

Speak hope into hard places.

May 08

Affirm yourself—you're listening.

May 09

Steady is powerful during storms.

May 10

Choose growth over giving up.

May 11

Support lightens the weight of disappointment.

May 12

You've overcome before—you will again.

May 13

Self-grace is a strength, not a weakness.

May 14

Shared resilience creates community.

May 15

Hope is a decision worth making.

May 16

Lead calmly through the chaos.

Positive Influence for Future Impact

May 17

Renewal begins with recommitment.

May 18

Have faith in the process.

May 19

Recovery requires time—not rushing.

May 20

You are stronger now than you were yesterday.

May 21

Learn something new —it keeps you growing.

May 22

*Ask with curiosity,
not certainty.*

May 23

Feedback is a mirror for growth.

May 24

Your habits are building your future.

May 25

Let inspiration shape your thinking.

May 26

Perfection isn't the goal—progress is.

May 27

Teach to deepen what you know.

May 28

Apply what you learn—make it real.

May 29

Encourage a mindset that sees possibility.

May 30

Growth is happening —even when it's quiet.

May 31

*Speak your truth—
kindly and clearly.*

June 01

*Align your actions
with your values.*

June 02

Use your voice to lift others.

June 03

Model what you believe.

June 04

Stand for something —even when it's hard.

June 05

Contribute to something bigger than yourself.

June 06

Collaboration creates lasting change.

June 07

Make space for everyone to belong.

June 08

Responsibility strengthens communities.

June 09

Your impact is felt— own it with care.

June 10

Honesty builds trust —even in the hard moments.

June 11

*Act with courage
when it matters most.*

June 12

*Let integrity lead—
even under pressure.*

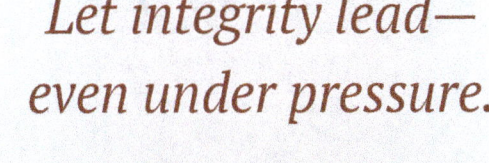

June 13

Ethical choices inspire ethical people.

June 14

Let your values guide your steps.

June 15

Give without expecting—serve from the heart.

June 16

Gratitude builds bridges.

June 17

See the unseen.
Thank the unthanked.

June 18

Humility strengthens every kind of leadership.

June 19

Giving adds meaning to life.

June 20

*Mentor by example—
it lasts longer.*

June 21

Empower others to lead.

June 22

Your influence echoes beyond today.

June 23

*Keep choosing action
that uplifts.*

June 24

Celebrate your growth—it's been earned.

June 25

Start each day with intention.

June 26

Encouragement can change a life.

June 27

Patience invites growth.

June 28

Kindness isn't weakness—it's wisdom.

June 29

Be consistent—it builds trust.

June 30

Appreciate the quiet helpers.

July 01

*Listen to understand,
not to reply.*

July 02

Help before being asked.

July 03

Choose understanding. Drop assumptions.

July 04

*Small choices build
great character.*

July 05

Encourage someone to keep going.

July 06

Model calm when stress rises.

July 07

Reflection protects reaction.

July 08

Reliability builds trust.

July 09

Speak truth with love.

July 10

Gratitude changes everything.

July 11

Affirm effort—it fuels progress.

July 12

Stay humble in success.

July 13

Be fully present—it matters.

July 14

Collaboration multiplies impact.

July 15

Be fair—it earns respect.

Positive Influence for Future Impact

July 16

Show yourself grace today.

July 17

Celebrate progress— not perfection.

July 18

Your example is someone's guide.

July 19

Reflect on how far you've come.

July 20

Your presence can transform a shared space.

July 21

Responsibility nurtures stronger communities.

July 22

Be the calm in the conflict.

July 23

Empathy honors perspectives beyond your own.

July 24

Serve quietly—legacy grows in humility.

July 25

Bridge builders create unity where division stood.

July 26

Use your voice to uplift the unheard.

July 27

Encouraging others sparks lasting growth.

July 28

Let ethics guide every decision.

July 29

You shape the atmosphere around you.

July 30

Lead with actions others want to follow.

July 31

Patience is a companion to growth.

August 01

Inclusion is an intentional choice.

August 02

Time builds trust—invest it.

August 03

*You are growing—
even if you can't see
it.*

August 04

Gratitude makes the ordinary extraordinary.

Positive Influence for Future Impact

August 05

Choose hope in moments of uncertainty.

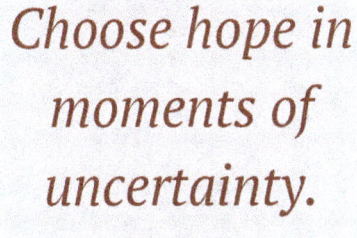

August 06

Responsibility empowers, not burdens.

August 07

*Stretch yourself—
serve beyond comfort.*

August 08

Contribute to the collective good—it matters.

August 09

A few kind words can shift the whole mood.

August 10

Patience welcomes learning with open arms.

August 11

Be mindful—your words ripple outward.

August 12

Kindness counts, even when unseen.

August 13

*Fairness builds trust
that lasts.*

August 14

Empathy bridges even the deepest gaps.

August 15

Service widens your circle of care.

August 16

Perseverance inspires more than success.

August 17

Choose optimism—it becomes a habit.

August 18

Daily habits shape your influence.

August 19

Accountability
supports real growth.

August 20

Grace can soothe even the tense moments.

August 21

Presence turns routine into meaning.

August 22

Listening builds stronger relationships.

August 23

Recognize effort—it fuels resilience.

August 24

Shared ownership empowers everyone.

August 25

Choose integrity when no one's watching.

August 26

Know what anchors you under pressure.

August 27

Collaboration multiplies what one alone cannot do.

August 28

Hope is the light that leads through uncertainty.

August 29

Consistency earns trust—day after day.

August 30

Small promises kept build big credibility.

August 31

You influence every space you enter.

September 01

Mistakes are stepping stones for growth.

September 02

*Lead with humility—
it deepens impact.*

September 03

Calm is a choice—and a strength.

Positive Influence for Future Impact

September 04

Believing in others unlocks their strength.

September 05

Celebrate the progress you often overlook.

September 06

Inspire others through your actions.

September 07

Intentionality fuels consistency.

September 08

Gratitude reframes even the hard days.

September 09

Let service be its own reward.

September 10

Your ethics shape your leadership.

September 11

Unity preserves dignity in disagreement.

September 12

Let values guide your approach to conflict.

September 13

Growth has its own timing—trust it.

September 14

Say it again—encouragement never gets old.

September 15

Hope is a deliberate choice.

September 16

Build trust through intentional presence.

Positive Influence for Future Impact

September 17

*Contribution
strengthens
community.*

September 18

Fairness fosters credibility over time.

September 19

Perseverance inspires shared strength.

September 20

Be present in the small moments—they matter.

September 21

Let your actions define your leadership.

September 22

Positive habits compound success.

September 23

Silent service still echoes.

September 24

Integrity becomes who you are—not what you do.

September 25

Belief in the future ignites progress.

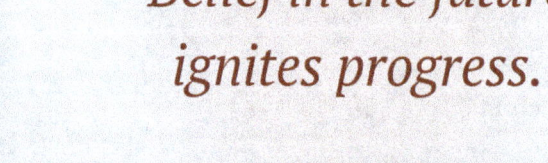

September 26

Emotional growth shows in how you respond.

September 27

Generosity expands your reach.

September 28

Encourage teamwork —it renews shared purpose.

September 29

Steady hearts calm chaotic days.

September 30

Consistency is the architecture of trust.

October 01

Your words may be someone's turning point.

October 02

Joy strengthens every act of service.

October 03

Respect sustains accountability.

October 04

You don't need a title to influence.

October 05

*Patience protects
what rush ruins.*

October 06

Resilience grows with every challenge faced.

October 07

Shared ownership brings stronger results.

October 08

Your energy shapes the room—bring it with care.

October 09

Let experience be your greatest teacher.

October 10

Empathy invites deeper understanding.

October 11

Show up with purpose in your community.

October 12

*Serve anonymously—
let the impact shine.*

October 13

*Hope is renewable—
use it often.*

October 14

Trust is built through small, steady steps.

October 15

Discipline is freedom in disguise.

October 16

Belief in others plants the seeds of growth.

October 17

Integrity must be renewed every day.

October 18

Endurance turns effort into legacy.

October 19

Positive culture begins with you.

October 20

Consistency magnifies every act of service.

October 21

Carry your lessons into tomorrow.

October 22

Vision turns hope into motion.

Positive Influence for Future Impact

October 23

Gratitude keeps joy alive.

Positive Influence for Future Impact

October 24

Your example is a quiet mentor.

Positive Influence for Future Impact

October 25

Commitment drives lasting change.

October 26

Patience nurtures goals worth waiting for.

October 27

Consistency is who you are becoming.

October 28

Mentorship shapes generations.

October 29

Encourage leadership in the quietest voices.

Positive Influence for Future Impact

October 30

Your habits build your tomorrow.

October 31

Purpose elevates even the ordinary.

November 01

Choose consistency, not convenience.

November 02

Resilience is contagious—share it.

November 03

Be someone's calm today.

November 04

Your words are seeds —speak with care.

November 05

You are building legacy every day.

November 06

*Serve from the soul—
not the spotlight.*

November 07

Invite others to reflect —it deepens impact.

November 08

Generosity multiplies your reach.

November 09

Act boldly—it inspires others.

November 10

Your values are your compass—follow them.

November 11

Your presence has power—use it wisely.

November 12

Your encouragement keeps others moving.

November 13

Gratitude never runs dry—draw from it often.

November 14

Mentorship builds future influence.

Positive Influence for Future Impact

November 15

Leadership is how you show up—not your title.

November 16

Discipline keeps your purpose alive.

November 17

Inspire others with your consistent action.

November 18

Let hope be your first reaction.

November 19

Integrity echoes beyond the moment.

November 20

Reflect on the miles you've walked.

November 21

Commit again to the journey forward.

Positive Influence for Future Impact

November 22

Prepare now for the influence ahead.

November 23

Invite someone to begin again.

November 24

Consistency is your greatest legacy.

November 25

Service defines true leadership.

November 26

Say thank you—mean it.

November 27

Be gentle with your growth.

November 28

Believe in what's possible.

November 29

Your influence touches more than you know.

Positive Influence for Future Impact

November 30

Commit to showing up with purpose.

December 01

Lead with your heart —people feel it.

December 02

Hope lasts longer than doubt.

December 03

Your legacy is in progress—keep going.

December 04

Encourage the next to carry the flame.

December 05

Lifelong influence begins with today's choice.

December 06

Celebrate how far you've come.

December 07

Begin again—with fresh intention.

December 08

Help others reflect on their growth.

December 09

Tiny habits shape big futures.

December 10

Support without control—true empowerment.

December 11

Humility protects influence.

December 12

Let your values lead the way.

Positive Influence for Future Impact

December 13

Your resilience lifts others.

December 14

Spend time where it truly matters.

December 15

Gratitude powers the next step.

December 16

Carry your wisdom forward.

December 17

*Keep becoming—
you're not done yet.*

December 18

Hope fuels perseverance.

December 19

Serve with intention today.

December 20

*Let integrity mark
every moment.*

December 21

Every action has influence—use it well.

December 22

Encouragement is a gift that grows.

December 23

Be patient—your goal is still unfolding.

December 24

Stay intentional—it keeps you grounded.

Positive Influence for Future Impact

December 25

Your legacy is what remains when you're gone.

December 26

Hope is the better choice—every time.

December 27

Inspire others to influence positively.

December 28

Gratitude is your daily anchor.

Positive Influence for Future Impact

December 29

Keep growing—you're built for it.

December 30

Be proud of who you've become.

December 31

Live the influence you've spent all year building.

www.ingramcontent.com/pod-product-compliance
Lightning Source LLC
Chambersburg PA
CBHW060404130626
46555CB00005B/1988